WORLD'S GREATEST
ORCHESTRAL, OPERA & BALLET THEMES
For Piano

57 Best-Loved Compositions by the Finest Composers

Selected and Arranged by
DAN FOX

D1609620

This collection of great music is drawn from the most memorable works of the finest composers. You'll find excerpts from the world's greatest symphonies, concertos, operas and ballets, as well as notable waltzes, marches and other instrumental music.

Included are themes from the symphonies of the great masters such as Haydn, Beethoven, Schubert, Brahms and Tchaikovsky. Famous themes from concertos are also represented, such as Rachmaninoff's *Rhapsody on a Theme by Paganini* and Gershwin's *Rhapsody in Blue.* You'll also find music from timeless ballets such as *Coppélia* and *Dance of the Hours,* as well as best-loved pieces from the operas of Mozart, Offenbach, Bizet, Verdi, Puccini and others. In addition, there are short paragraphs full of interesting and little-known facts about each of the selections.

We're sure that this collection will become a favorite, providing many hours of enjoyment at the keyboard.

WYNDHAM CITY
LIBRARY SERVICE
P.O. BOX 197
WERRIBEE VIC. 3030

Copyright © MMVI by Alfred Publishing Co., Inc.
All rights reserved.   Printed in USA.
ISBN-10: 0-7390-4379-X
ISBN-13: 978-0-7390-4379-O

Alfred

$28.50

CONTENTS

George Gershwin was on top of the world in 1928. His *Rhapsody in Blue, Concerto in F,* and many successful Broadway shows had made him an international celebrity, sought out by composers like Maurice Ravel, Darius Milhaud, and Sergei Prokofiev. Gershwin actually was in the "City of Light" when he wrote this theme from his orchestral suite *An American in Paris,* later made into a ballet and a hit movie starring Gene Kelly.

AN AMERICAN IN PARIS™
(Blues Theme)

By George Gershwin
(1898–1937)

Moderately slow, with a steady beat

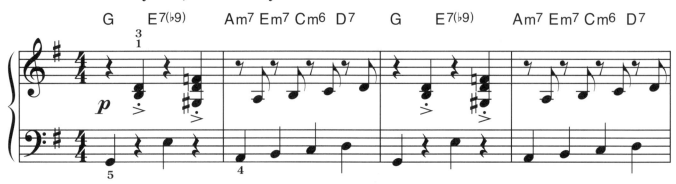

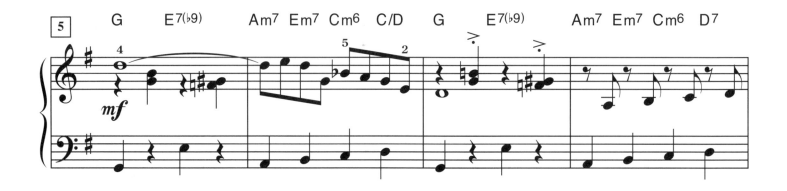

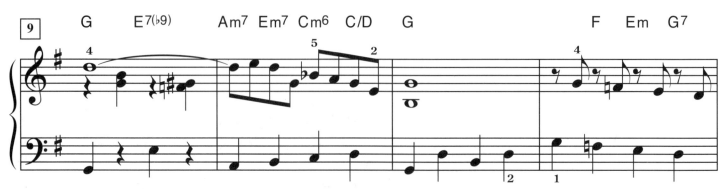

© 1929 (Renewed) WB Music Corp.
This Arrangement © 2006 WB Music Corp.
AN AMERICAN IN PARIS™ is a trademark of the George Gershwin Family Trust
GERSHWIN® and GEORGE GERSHWIN® are registered trademarks of Gershwin Enterprises
All Rights Reserved

Enrique Granados, who the great cellist Pablo Casals once called "the Schubert of Spain," was still a young man when his Spanish Dances made him famous in the 1890s. His career was cut tragically short during World War I when he and his wife both drowned after a German submarine torpedoed the ship on which they were traveling. The title of this piece refers to a district in Spain.

ANDALUZA
(Spanish Dance No. 5)

Enrique Granados
(1867–1916)

Andantino (not too fast, but not dragging)

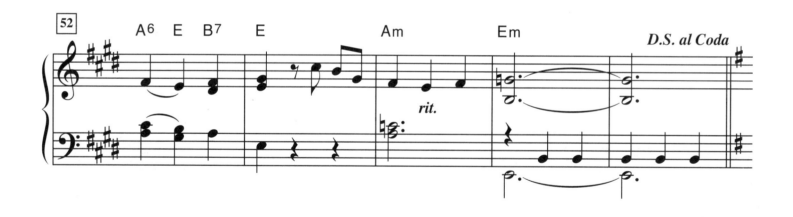

Since being used in Stanley Kubrick's classic 1968 science-fiction film, this theme has become perhaps the most famous opening measures in any piece of classical music. German composer Richard Strauss left behind a legacy of hundreds of works, from songs to massive orchestral tone poems.

ALSO SPRACH ZARATHUSTRA

Richard Strauss
(1864–1949)

Composed in 1871, this lovely melody became the slow movement in the composer's *String Quartet in D.* Although Tchaikovsky's private life was filled with torment and despair, no trace of either can be found in this sunny piece. *Andante cantabile* means "not fast, with a singing tone."

ANDANTE CANTABILE

Peter Ilyich Tchaikovsky
(1840–1893)

This famous excerpt is from Norwegian composer Edvard Grieg's "Peer Gynt Suite," a series of descriptive pieces cataloguing the adventures of Peer Gynt as he travels the world. Anitra is the temptress who attempts to keep Peer Gynt captive to her charms.

ANITRA'S DANCE

(from *Peer Gynt*)

Edvard Grieg
(1843–1907)

It might be difficult to take *Il Trovatore* seriously after seeing the Marx Brothers' lampoon *A Night at the Opera*. But because of its glorious music (and in spite of an extremely confusing plot) *Il Trovatore* has always been a favorite of opera fans. Its most famous tune is this one that features gypsies banging on anvils. On stage, electric currents make sure that the sparks fly.

ANVIL CHORUS
(from the opera *Il Trovatore*)

Giuseppe Verdi
(1813–1901)

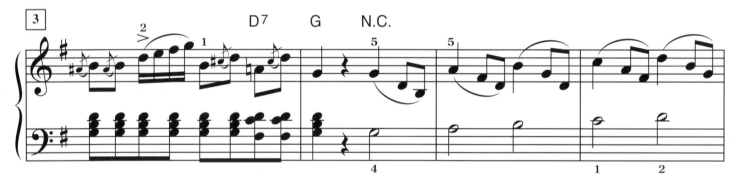

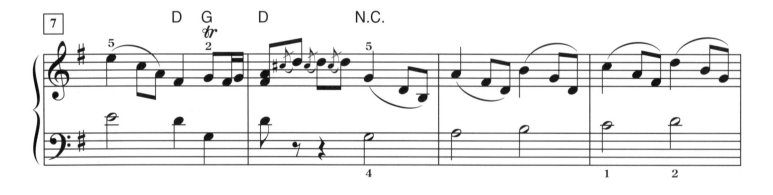

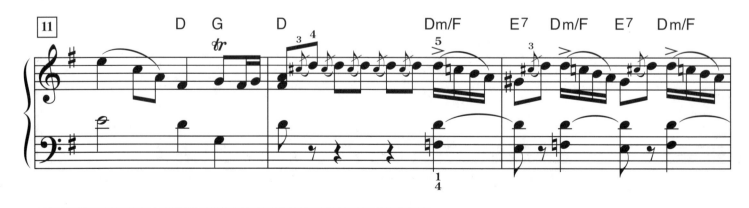

Rarely in the history of music has an artist so captured an era as did Austrian composer Johann Strauss, Jr. His waltzes capture the light-hearted gaiety so characteristic of 19th-century Vienna when it was the center of European musical life.

Artist's Life

Johann Strauss, Jr.
(1825–1899)

Offenbach was one of the most prolific composers that ever lived. In the middle of the 19th century, nobody's music was more popular in France than his, and he turned out a continuous stream of witty operettas that slyly made fun of the pretensions of Napoleon III and his corrupt court. A *barcarolle* is a piece of music that imitates the songs sung by Venetian gondoliers.

BARCAROLLE
(from *The Tales of Hoffman*)

Jacques Offenbach
(1819–1880)

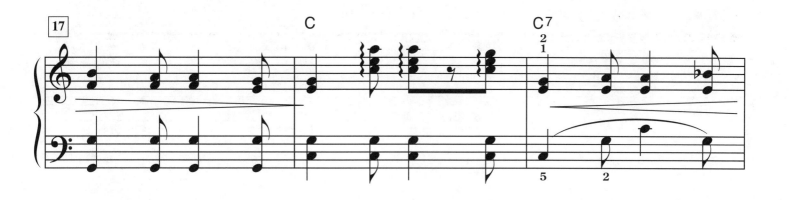

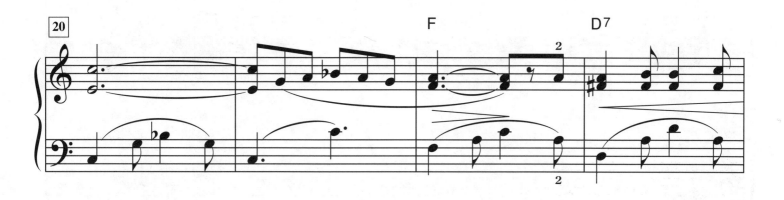

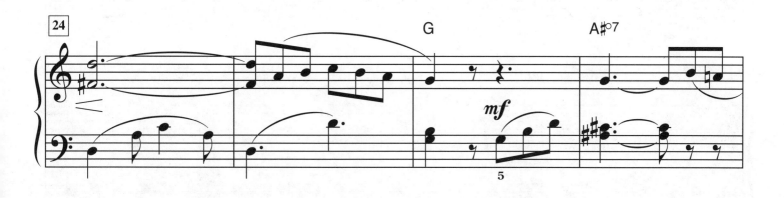

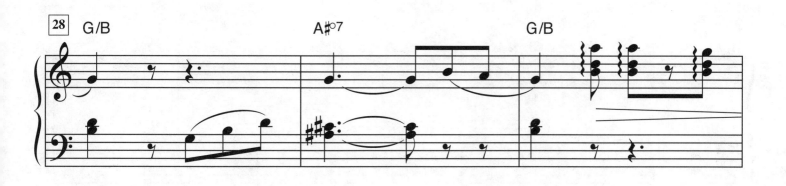

This is probably the most famous waltz in the world. It celebrates the Danube, Europe's second longest river. Under the mistaken impression that he was the composer, someone once asked Johannes Brahms to autograph a copy of *The Blue Danube* waltz. He wrote: "Regrettably *not* by your humble servant, Johannes Brahms."

THE BLUE DANUBE

Johann Strauss, Jr.
(1825–1899)

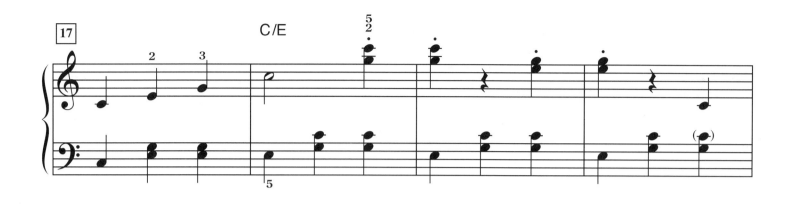

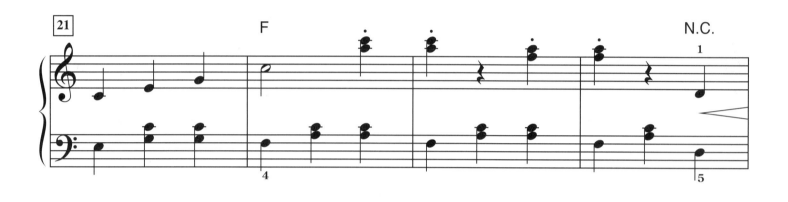

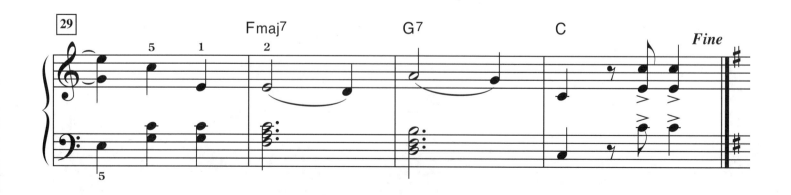

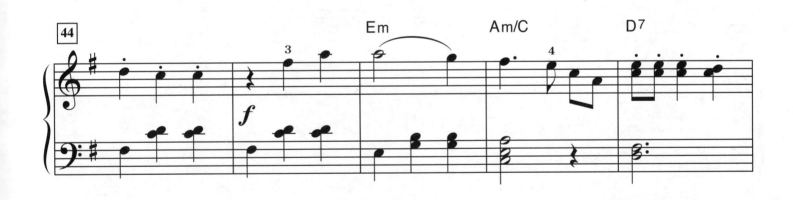

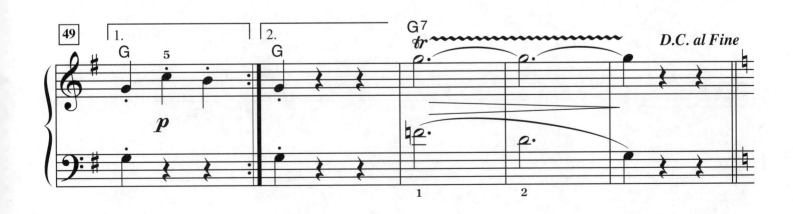

Because the opening theme to his monumental 5th symphony was so short (only four notes), the musicians who first heard it thought it was one of Beethoven's famous musical jokes. Over a hundred years later, during World War II, this theme symbolized the Allies' "V for Victory," because the music resembles Morse code for the letter "V" *(dot–dot–dot–DASH).*

Symphony No. 5

(Opening Theme)

Ludwig van Beethoven
(1770–1827)

Bright and spirited

Along with Beethoven's 2nd symphony, this work, nicknamed the "Pastoral Symphony," is one of the great composer's most charming and bucolic. In the score, various themes are labeled "Idyll by the brook," "Storm," and this one, "Shepherd's Song," which suggests the peacefulness that returns to the countryside after the storm has passed.

SYMPHONY No. 6
(Shepherd's Song)

Ludwig van Beethoven
(1770–1827)

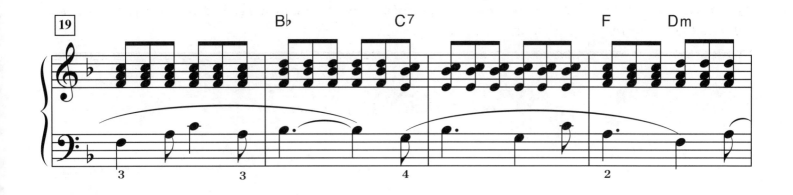

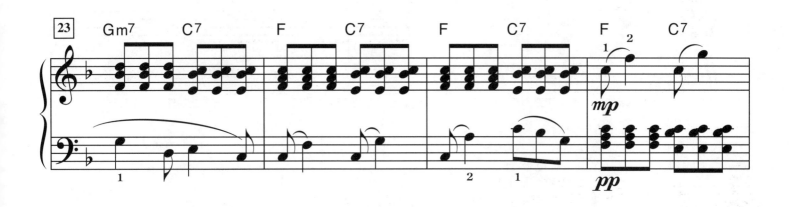

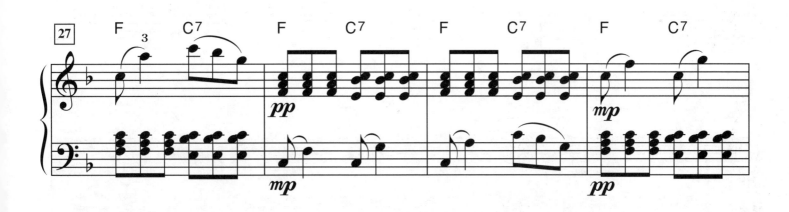

Beethoven had become completely deaf by the time he wrote his 7th symphony. The second movement, a theme and variations, actually includes two different themes. The basic idea is presented in measures 1–16. The counter-melody enters in measure 17, just below the melody in the right hand.

SYMPHONY NO. 7
(2nd Movement Theme)

Ludwig van Beethoven
(1770–1827)

One of the things that makes Brahms' music so wonderfully interesting is his use of shifting accents. In the melody below, notice how the pick-up and the first measure divide the notes with four beats and two beats, rather than a less interesting 3 + 3. In measure 24 and other similar places, the accents make the second beat seem like the downbeat. Measures 31–34 sound like six measures of 2/4, rather than four measures of 3/4, an effect called *hemiola*.

SYMPHONY No. 3

(3rd Movement Theme)

Johannes Brahms
(1833–1897)

Offenbach had arrived in Paris from his native Alsace in 1833. Although he had neither money nor connections, his talent soon made him the toast of Paris. His specialty was satirizing well-known Greek myths, making them relevant to the Parisian audiences of that time. The "can can" was a naughty stage dance that featured a lot of high-kicking girls, flashing glimpses of their lacy undergarments.

CAN CAN

(from *Orpheus in the Underworld*)

Jacques Offenbach
(1819–1880)

Originally written in 1916, this march became famous after it was used in the 1957 film *The Bridge on the River Kwai,* a film about British prisoners of war being held by the Japanese during World War II.

COLONEL BOGEY

Kenneth J. Alford
(1881–1945)

This waltz comes from the ballet of the same name, written by French composer Léo Delibes. The composer based his ballet on a story by E. T. A. Hoffman. The plot of *Coppélia* concerns the fantastic Dr. Coppélius, whose life-like dolls have an effect on a pair of young lovers. First performed in Paris in 1870, the ballet has become a staple of the repertoire.

Coppélia Waltz

Léo Delibes
(1836–1891)

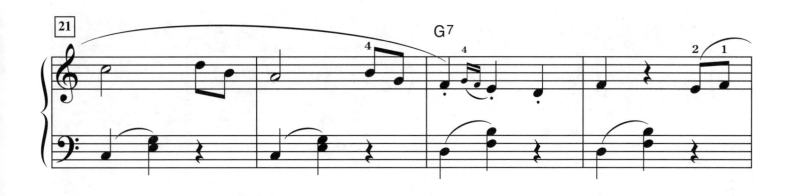

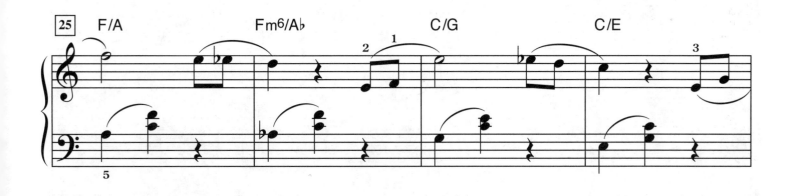

Although Amilcare Ponchielli was a serious composer, he created this piece of music that people seem to love to make fun of. First there was the Walt Disney animated film *Fantasia,* which portrayed ungainly elephants and dainty hippopotami dancing to the music. Then in the 1950s, it was mercilessly parodied as "Hello Muddah, Hello Fadduh." Ironically, this music comes from the serious opera *La Gioconda,* which is a melodramatic work full of murder and betrayal.

DANCE OF THE HOURS

(from *La Gioconda*)

Amilcare Ponchielli
(1834–1886)

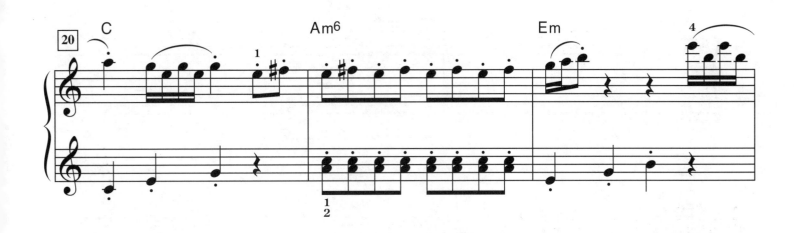

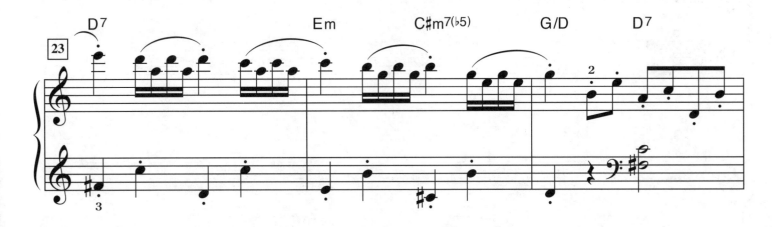

The title means "A Little Night Music." Mozart was at the height of his powers in 1787, and busy working on his operatic masterpiece *Don Giovanni* when he wrote this charming work. Each of the four movements is a little gem, and the piece remains one of the great composer's most popular works.

EINE KLEINE NACHTMUSIK
(Opening Theme)

Wolfgang Amadeus Mozart
(1756–1791)

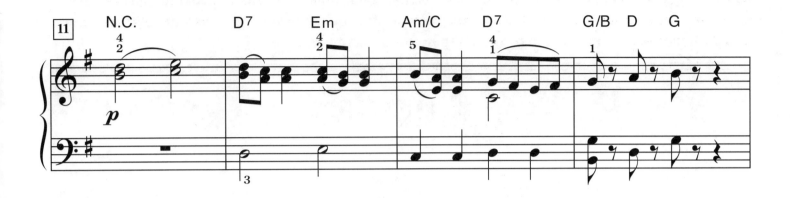

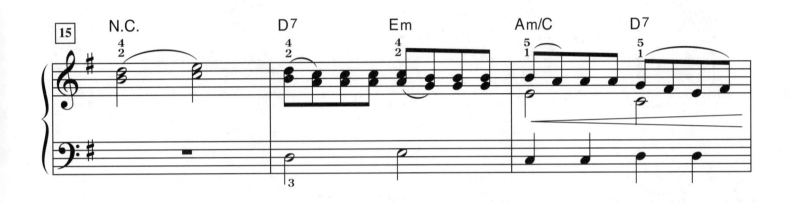

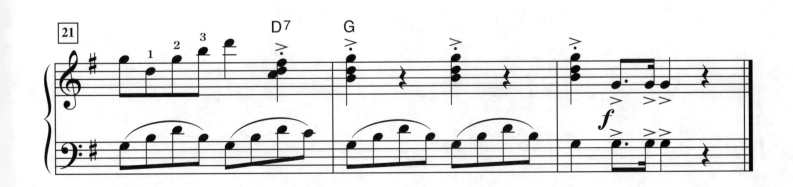

Although the critics sometimes accused him of writing salon music (akin to classical "elevator music"), French composer Jules Massenet was a serious composer who turned out popular operas, such as *Manon* and *Thaïs,* which are full of beautiful melodies such as this one. An *elegie* is a melancholic piece of music, often written to honor someone's death.

Elegie

Jules Massenet
(1842–1912)

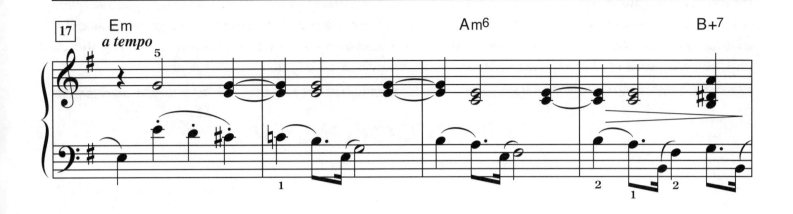

No, we're not talking about the pop singer who took his name. *This* Engelbert Humperdinck was a German composer whose opera *Hänsel and Gretel* is based on the fairy tale about two children abandoned in a forest, who narrowly escape from a wicked witch. In a touching scene, the frightened children huddle together as night falls and sing this prayer to beg the angels for protection.

EVENING PRAYER
(from the Opera *Hänsel and Gretel*)

Engelbert Humperdinck
(1854–1921)

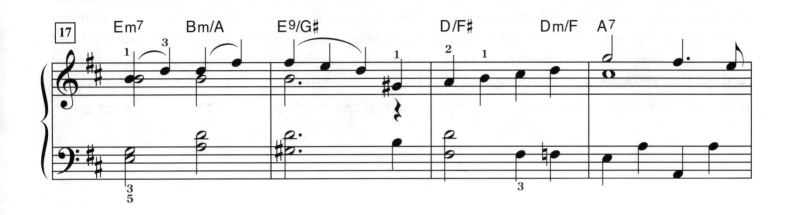

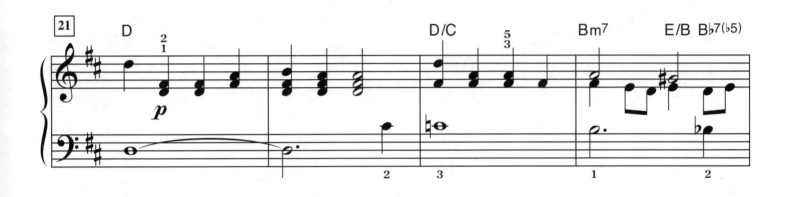

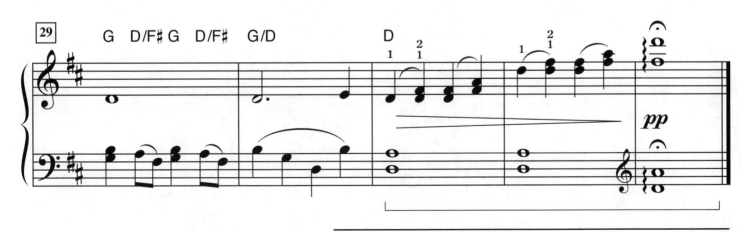

French composer Charles Gounod is best remembered for his church music and his operas, especially *Faust,* which is still performed regularly around the world. Gounod was also capable of writing lighter music, such as this mock funeral march for a puppet. Alfred Hitchcock—famed director of suspense and horror films—liked the piece's undertone of menace so much that he used it as the theme song for his television series.

FUNERAL MARCH OF A MARIONETTE

Charles Gounod
(1818–1893)

In order to celebrate the opening of the Suez Canal, the Viceroy of Egypt commissioned Verdi to write an opera about his country. *Aïda,* a melodrama of divided loyalties set in the time of the pharaohs, was a huge success when it finally premiered in 1871, and has remained one of the most popular of Verdi's many great operas. This march is played when the hero returns triumphantly from war.

GRAND MARCH
(from the Opera *Aïda*)

Giuseppe Verdi
(1813–1901)

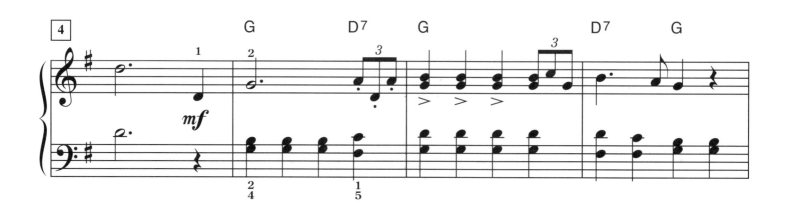

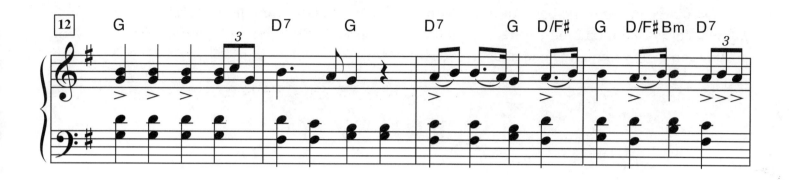

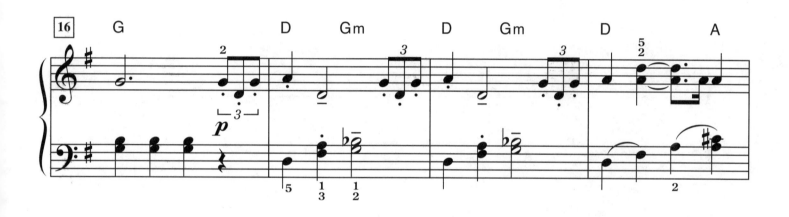

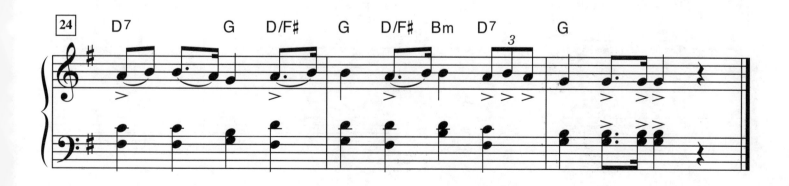

Italian composer Pietro Mascagni thought so little of the chances for his opera *Cavalleria Rusticana* (Rustic Chivalry), that he had put it away in a drawer and forgotten about it. However, his wife knew its great potential and entered it in a contest. Not only did it win, the opera was given a full production in 1890 and has had a lasting success.

INTERMEZZO
(from the Opera *Cavalleria Rusticana*)

Pietro Mascagni
(1863–1945)

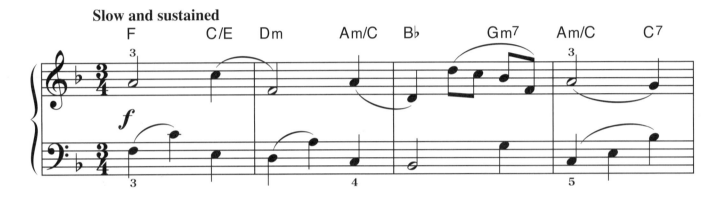

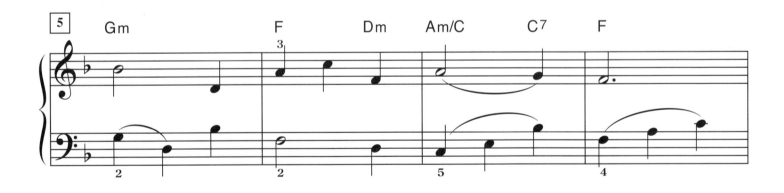

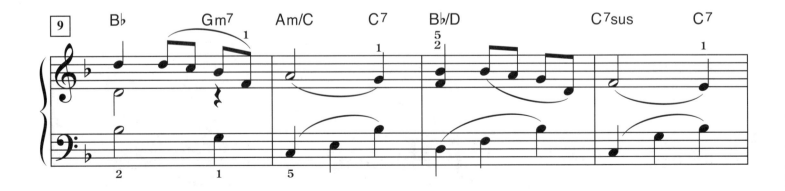

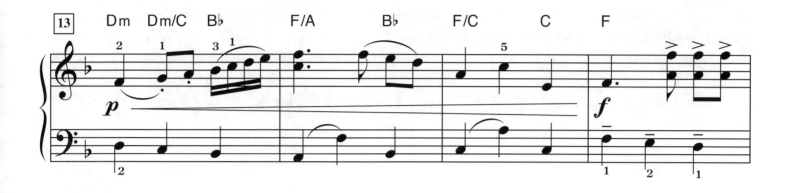

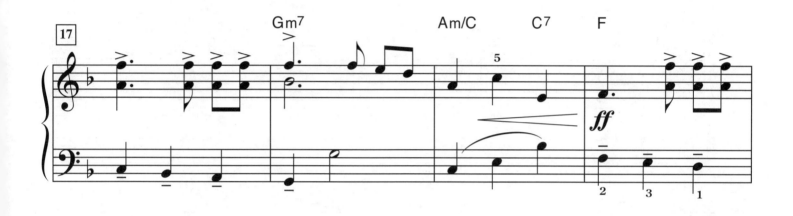

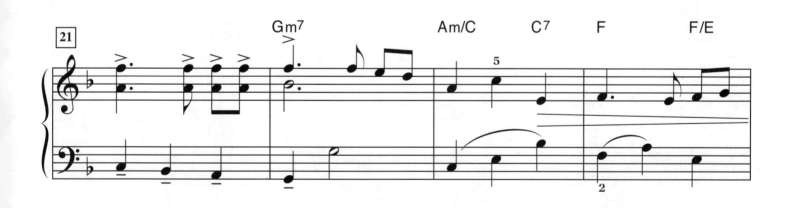

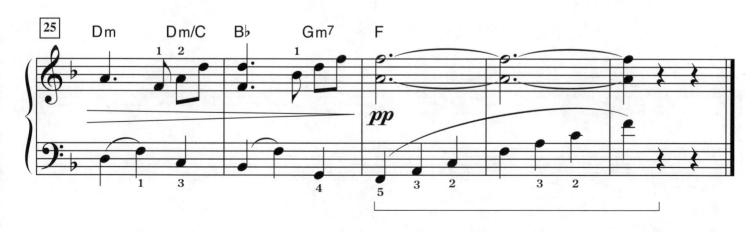

Like *Anitra's Dance,* (also in this book) this is one of the descriptive pieces from the *Peer Gynt Suite,* one of Grieg's most popular works. It should be played rather like a march, but as it gets louder and speeds up, the music becomes increasingly ominous, reaching its terrifying climax on the diminished 7th chords in measures 25–26 and 29–32.

IN THE HALL OF THE MOUNTAIN KING
(from *Peer Gynt*)

Edvard Grieg
(1843–1907)

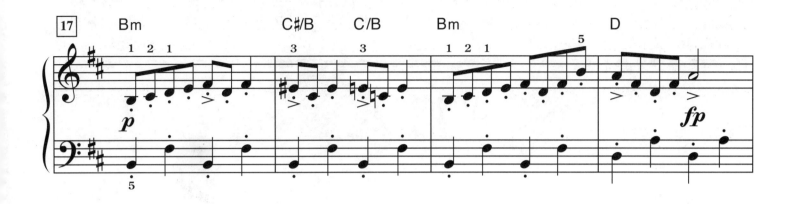

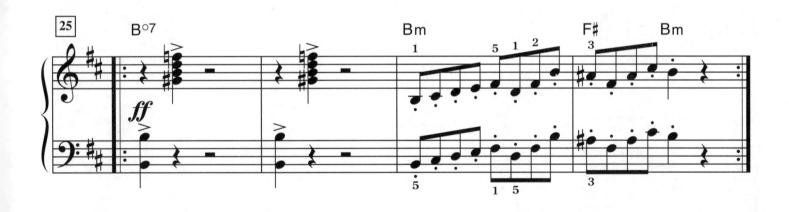

In these days of instant gratification, it seems incredible that Brahms worked on this symphony for 22 years. The wait was well worth it, however, for this is a masterpiece that some have jokingly, but admiringly called "Beethoven's 10th Symphony."

SYMPHONY NO. 1
(4th Movement Theme)

Johannes Brahms
(1833–1897)

La Belle Hélène (Beautiful Helen) refers to Helen of Troy, whose beauty was the cause of the Trojan War. Like many of Offenbach's works, this one uses Greek mythology to satirize the foibles of the French Second Empire. Napoleon III had taken over after the disturbances of 1848, and had himself crowned in 1852. His corrupt regime collapsed after a humiliating military defeat in 1870 by the Prussians, during which the emperor himself was captured.

LA BELLE HÉLÈNE WALTZ

Jacques Offenbach
(1819–1880)

Mozart's opera *Don Giovanni* tells the story of a nobleman who has been with so many women that his servant has to keep track of their names in a notebook. In this scene, Don Giovanni sings, "Là ci darem la mano" ("Put your hand in mine") to Zerlina, a pretty peasant girl. Mozart was composing music at the age of four, had perfect pitch, and played several instruments superbly. He left behind an enormous body of work, composed in his 35 short years. He died in 1791 and was buried in a mass grave.

LÀ CI DAREM LA MANO
(from the Opera *Don Giovanni*)

Wolfgang Amadeus Mozart
(1756–1791)

Men who lie to women to get their way have been known since the dawn of history, but it took French author Victor Hugo to make a successful play out of it. Verdi based his opera *Rigoletto* on Hugo's play. The story is a dark tale of the betrayal of an innocent girl, and a father's revenge gone horribly wrong. This is the best-known aria from the opera, in which the handsome seducer excuses his behavior by mockingly labeling all women as fickle.

LA DONNA È MOBILE
(from the Opera *Rigoletto*)

Giuseppe Verdi
(1813–1901)

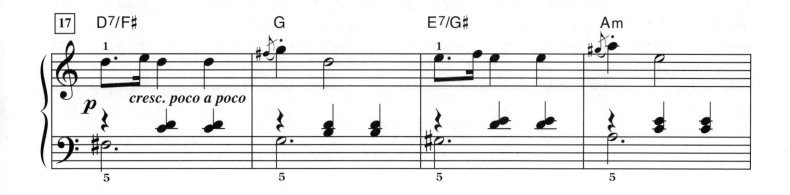

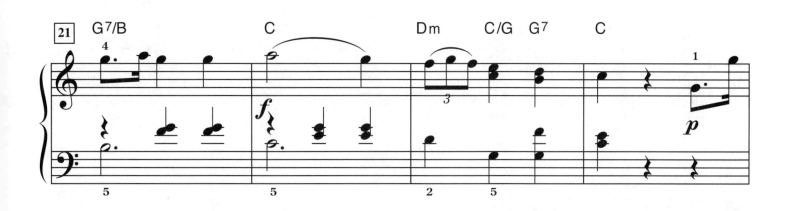

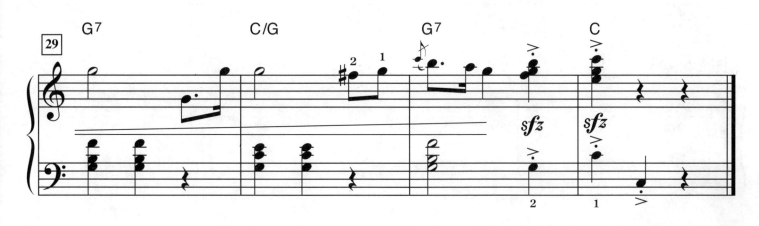

Czech composer Dvořák spent several years teaching, performing and composing in the United States. His Ninth Symphony, subtitled "From the New World," is the composer's best-known and most often performed work. Although it is supposedly based on American themes, it sounds much more Bohemian than American. (Bohemia is a district in central Europe that is now part of the Czech Republic.)

LARGO
(from the "New World" Symphony)

Antonín Dvořák
(1841–1904)

Rimsky-Korsakov was one of the most important composers of the 19th century. *Scheherazade* is a tone poem based on stories from *The Arabian Nights*. In this story, the beautiful Scheherazade avoids beheading by telling the king stories each night, but leaving them unfinished until the next day. She continues for "a thousand and one nights" until the king relents and they live happily ever after.

LOVE THEME
(from *Scheherazade*)

Nicolai Rimsky-Korsakov
(1844–1908)

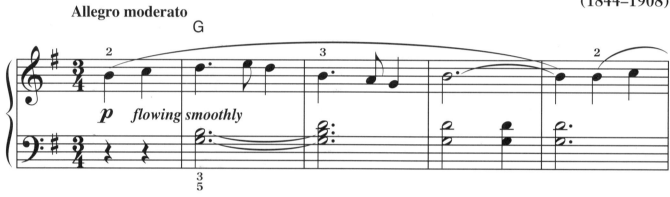

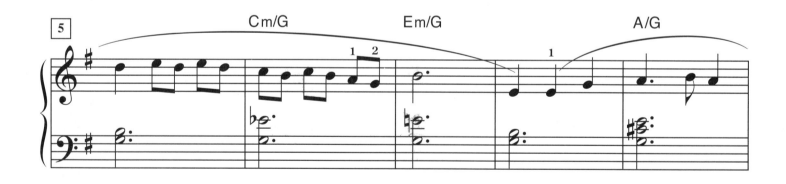

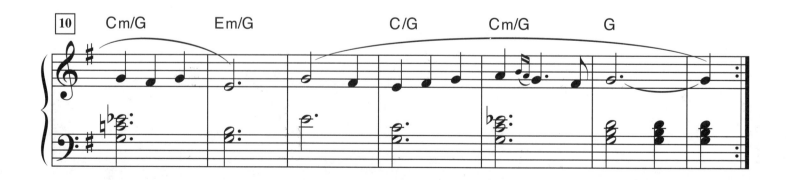

French author Alphonse Daudet's 1872 play *L'Arlésienne* (The Girl from Arles) is about life in Provençe, a district in south central France. Fellow Frenchman Georges Bizet was asked to write incidental music for the play, and drew much of his inspiration from Provençal folk songs, including this march which dates from the Middle Ages.

MARCH OF THE KINGS
(from *L'Arlésienne*)

Georges Bizet
(1838–1875)

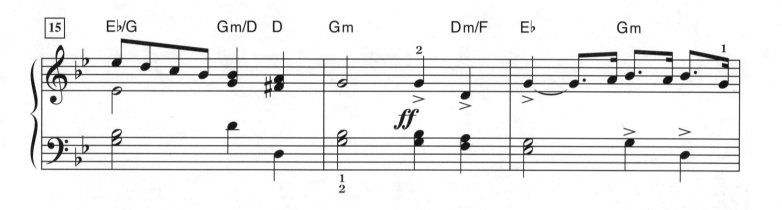

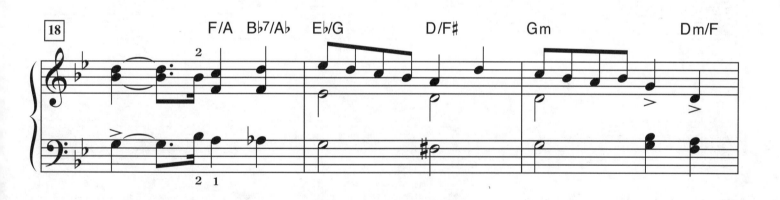

There was already a successful opera by Giovanni Paisiello based on Beaumarchais' satirical *The Barber of Seville* when Gioacchino Rossini decided to use the same French play as the basis of his opera. Unfortunately for Paisiello, Rossini's opera was a stunning masterpiece, and Paisiello's earlier work fell into obscurity. The mazurka is a 19th-century dance in which the second beat of the measure is accented.

MAZURKA
(from *The Barber of Seville*)

Gioacchino Rossini
(1792–1868)

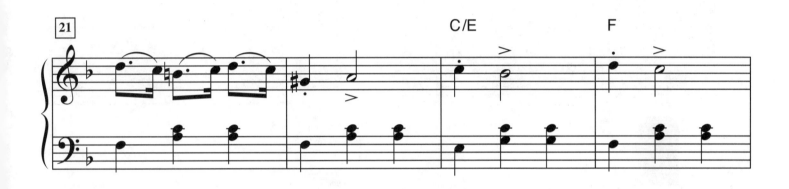

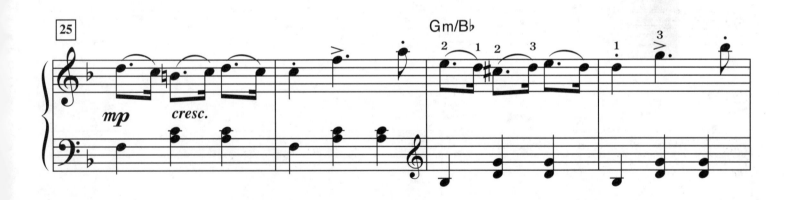

Although German composer Friedrich von Flotow cannot be considered of the first rank, he did have a great gift for melody. This piece, from his opera *Martha,* is the most famous. Flotow composed ballets, orchestral works, chamber music, songs and operas.

M'APPARI TUTT' AMOR
(from *Martha*)

Friedrich von Flotow
(1812–1883)

Puccini's *La Boheme* (The Bohemian) is an opera about poor artists and the women they love in early 19th-century Paris. In the story, Musetta has broken up with Marcello and is now with Alcindoro, a rich, older man. They all happen to meet at a café where Musetta realizes that she still loves Marcello, and sings this waltz to get him back. Marcello is once again entranced and leaves with the girl, leaving Alcindoro to pick up the check!

Musetta's Waltz
(from *La Boheme*)

Giacomo Puccini
(1858–1924)

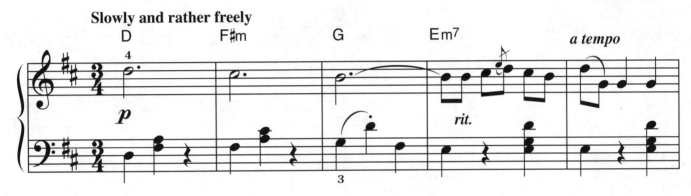

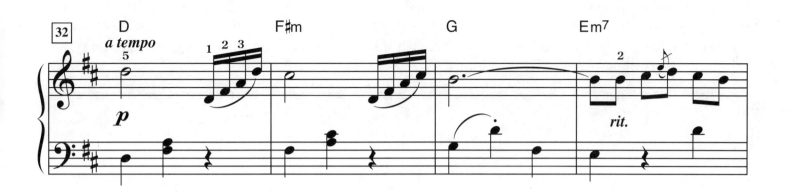

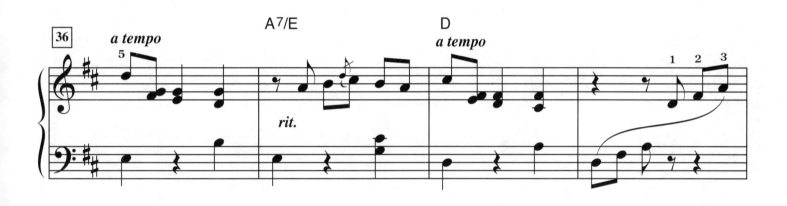

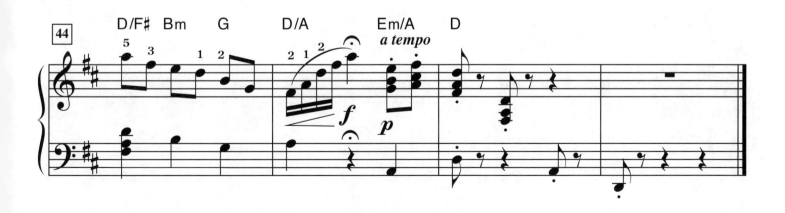

Completed in 1823 when Beethoven was completely deaf, the monumental Ninth Symphony goes far beyond the Classical symphonies of Mozart and Haydn. After three powerful and brooding movements, the finale brings in four soloists and a huge choir to sing the magnificent *Ode to Joy*. Virtually every important composer of the 19th century (especially Wagner, Schumann and Brahms) was influenced by this symphony.

ODE TO JOY
(from *Symphony No. 9*)

Ludwig van Beethoven
(1770–1827)

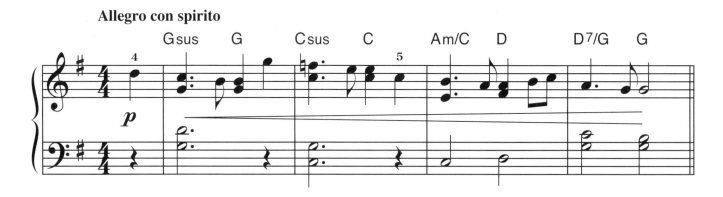

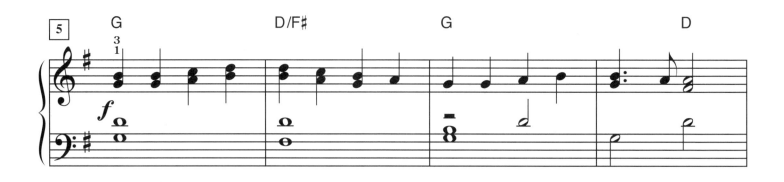

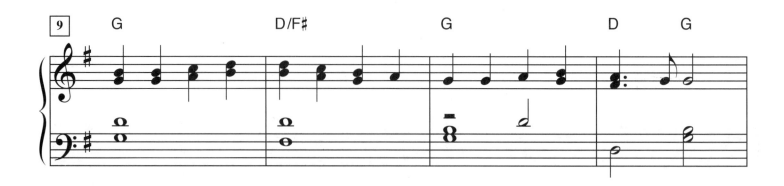

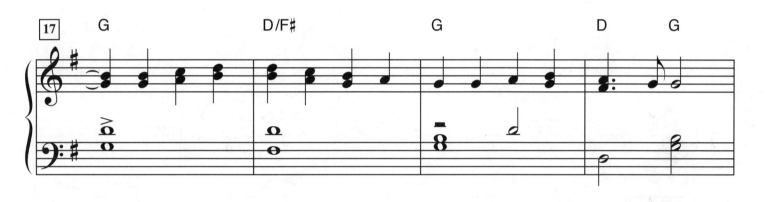

This aria is from an opera that features a comic story about how the wily Gianni Schicchi puts one over on the greedy relatives of a recently deceased rich man. This short one-act opera is part of a trilogy that also includes the religious drama *Suor Angelica* (Sister Angelica), and the murder story *Il Tabarro* (The Cloak). *O mio babbino caro* is sung by Gianni Schicchi's daughter Lauretta, and is one of Puccini's most beautiful arias.

O MIO BABBINO CARO
(from the Opera *Gianni Schicchi*)

Giacomo Puccini
(1858–1924)

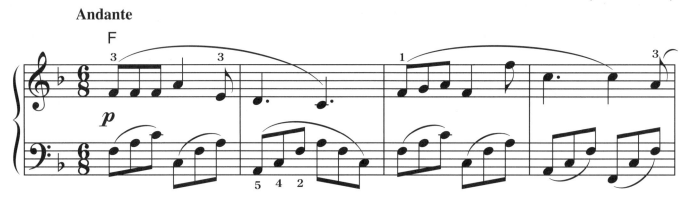

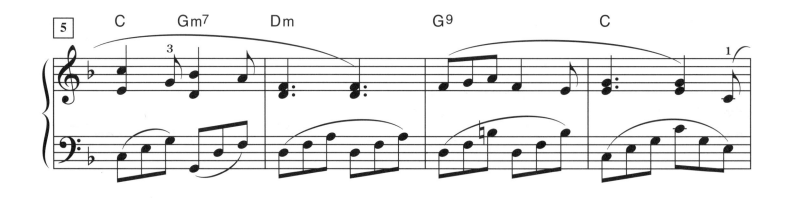

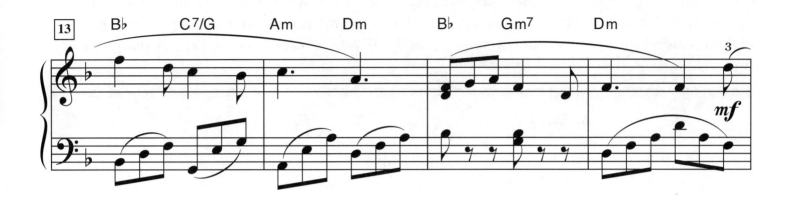

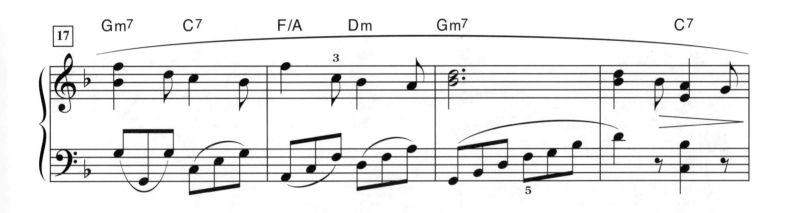

It's almost as though Tchaikovsky foresaw his own death when he subtitled his Sixth Symphony "Pathétique," a French word meaning "sad" or "deserving of tears." The first performances were met with indifference by his jaded audience, and only a few months later he was dead of cholera, a disease caused by drinking contaminated water. Only after several years did the symphony attain the popularity that it enjoys to this day.

PATHÉTIQUE SYMPHONY
(1st Movement Theme)

Peter Ilyich Tchaikovsky
(1840–1893)

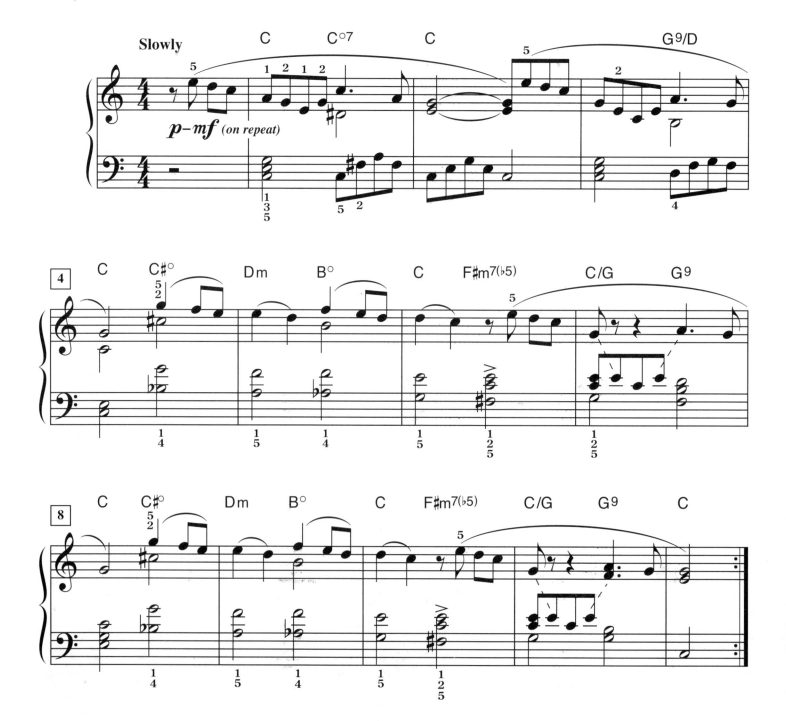

In his twenties, Russian composer Sergei Rachmaninoff experienced a deep depression that made it impossible for him to compose, play or conduct. He turned to an experimental treatment involving hypnosis, pioneered by a psychologist named Nikolai Dahl. The treatments were successful, and in gratitude, Rachmaninoff dedicated his second piano concerto to Dahl.

PIANO CONCERTO NO. 2
(1st Movement Theme)

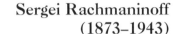

Sergei Rachmaninoff
(1873–1943)

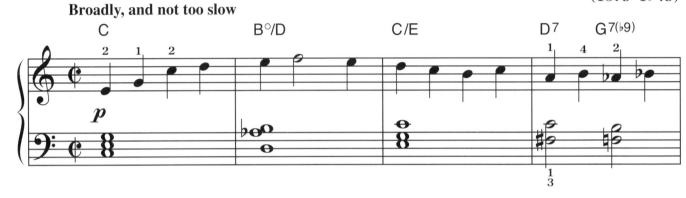

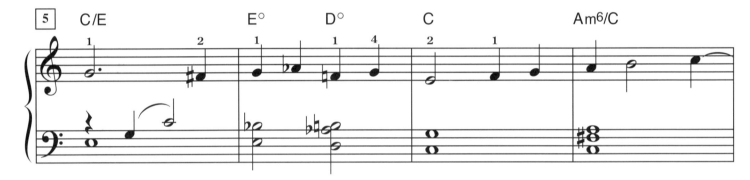

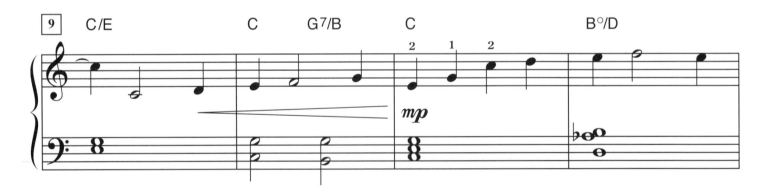

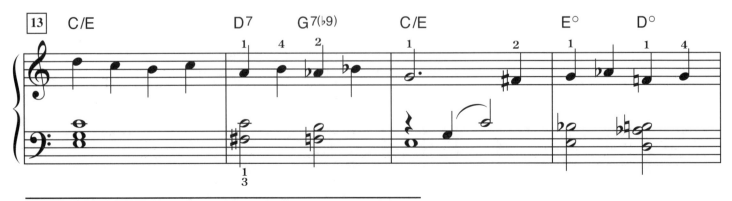

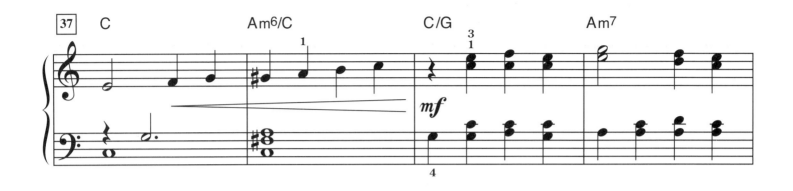

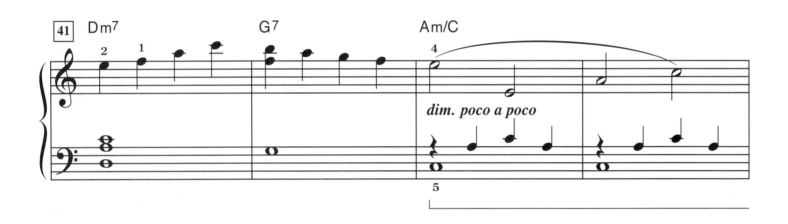

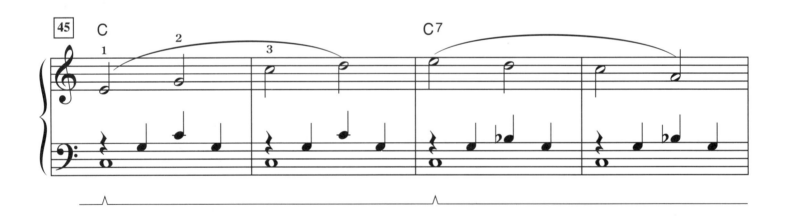

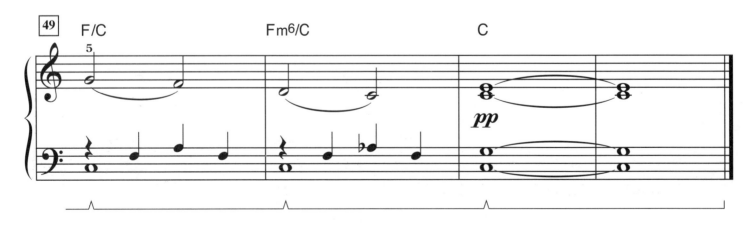

The *pavane* was a slow and solemn dance that was very popular in the 16th and 17th centuries. Fauré, the composer of this hauntingly beautiful *Pavane,* was also the teacher of the great composer Maurice Ravel (1875–1937), among others.

PAVANE

Gabriel Fauré
(1845–1924)

In 1924, bandleader Paul Whiteman asked George Gershwin—already the darling of Broadway for his jazzy show tunes—to compose a piece for an upcoming New York City concert. The result was the world-famous *Rhapsody in Blue,* which has probably been performed more times than any other piece of American concert music.

RHAPSODY IN BLUE™
(Main Theme)

By George Gershwin
(1898–1937)

© 1929 (Renewed) WB Music Corp.
This Arrangement © 2006 WB Music Corp.
RHAPSODY IN BLUE™ is a trademark of the George Gershwin Family Trust
GERSHWIN® and GEORGE GERSHWIN® are registered trademarks of Gershwin Enterprises
All Rights Reserved

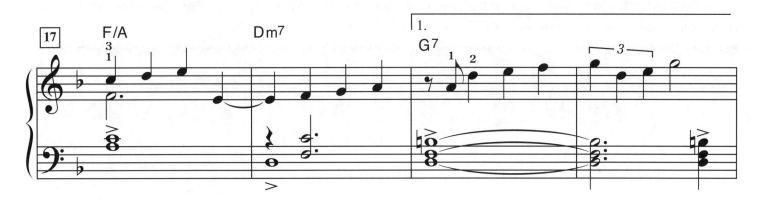

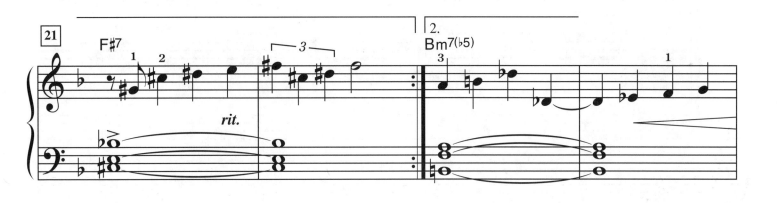

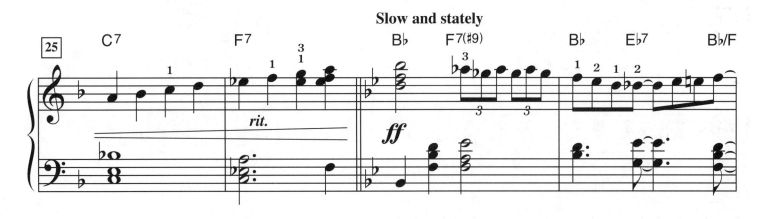

Any competent composer can take a tune and turn it upside down, but it took the genius of Sergei Rachmaninoff to come up with this glorious melody, along with 23 other variations on a famous theme by Italian composer Niccolò Paganini (1782–1840).

RHAPSODY ON A THEME BY PAGANINI
(18th Variation)

By Sergei Rachmaninoff
(1873–1943)

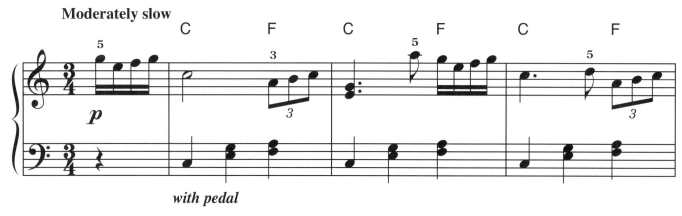

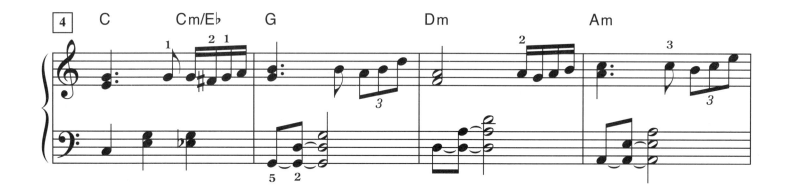

© 1934 by Charles Foley, Inc.
Copyright Renewed
All Rights Assigned to and Administered by BOOSEY & HAWKES MUSIC PUBLISHERS LTD. (Publishing)
and ALFRED PUBLISHING CO., INC. (Print)
All Rights Reserved

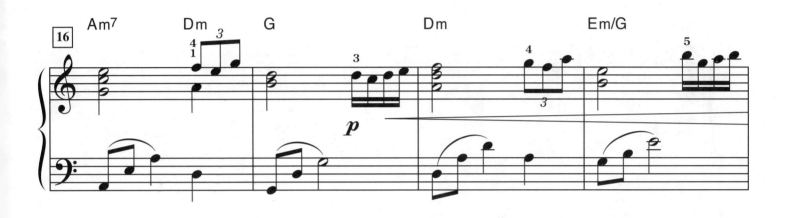

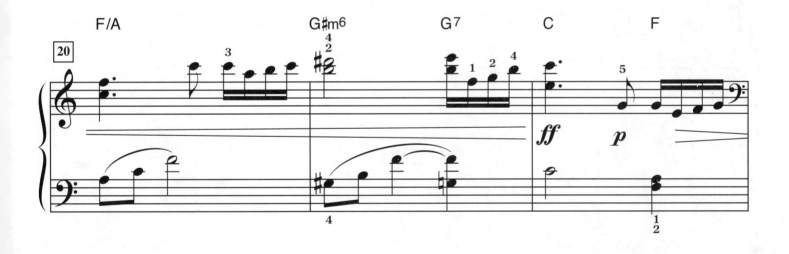

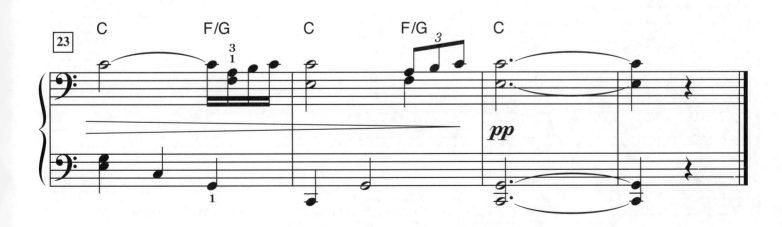

Dating back to the Middle Ages, wandering minstrels sang about star-crossed lovers from families that were mortal enemies. This story has been the inspiration for many works of art, including William Shakespeare's immortal play, *Romeo and Juliet.* Tchaikovsky was undoubtedly attracted to the story because of its possibilities for dramatic music. He called his interpretation "Overture—Fantasy."

Love Theme from

ROMEO AND JULIET

(Overture—Fantasy)

Peter Ilyich Tchaikovsky
(1840–1893)

King Louis XIV enjoyed a very long reign (1643–1715) and was responsible for making France a major power in the world. This *rondeau* is by a court composer to Louis XIV, Jean-Joseph Mouret. He and his music had been pretty much forgotten when PBS chose the Rondeau as the theme for its excellent show, *Masterpiece Theater.* A *rondeau* is a medieval French song with instrumental accompaniment.

RONDEAU
("Masterpiece Theater" Theme)

Jean-Joseph Mouret
(1682–1738)

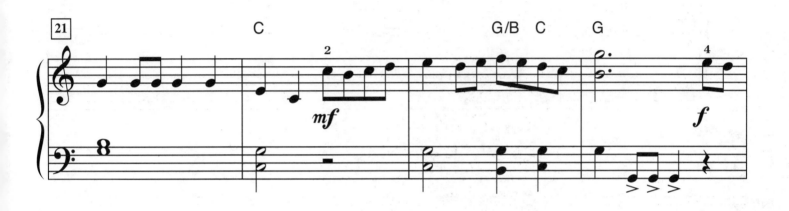

Franz Joseph Haydn had a successful career until his death at the ripe old age (for those times) of 77. He was a generous man who often called attention to younger composers including Mozart, whom he praised as being "the greatest composer known to me." He also gave lessons to the young Beethoven. Besides composing 104 symphonies and countless other works, Haydn perfected the form of the string quartet. This famous serenade comes from his String Quartet in F, Op. 3, No. 5.

SERENADE

Franz Joseph Haydn
(1732–1809)

Perhaps the greatest writer of classical songs that ever lived, Franz Schubert wrote over 600 songs in his pitifully short life of only 31 years. He also turned out wonderful chamber music, 10 superb symphonies, 6 masses, and innumerable works for the piano. He lived in the early days of the Romantic era, and was one of that period's defining composers. His famous *Serenade* was set to a poem by German poet Ludwig Rellstab, but was never published during the composer's lifetime.

SERENADE

Franz Schubert
(1797–1828)

Italian composer, pianist, and romantic icon Enrico Toselli was already well known in Europe when he wrote this lovely *Serenade*. Originally scored for string quartet, it was transcribed for the piano by the composer himself and became his most popular piece. Soon after its publication in 1907, Toselli eloped with the rich and beautiful Princess Luisa of Saxony, causing a sensational scandal in those pre-World War I days of Victorian morality.

Serenade

Enrico Toselli
(1883–1926)

When the waltz first became popular in the early 1800s, it was considered just a little naughty. Imagine that... people actually touching while they danced! Everyone went "waltz crazy," and soon virtually every composer was writing dozens of waltzes. Émile Waldteufel, a French composer known for his waltzes and polkas, combined the passion of the times for both waltzing and ice skating, and created this piece, which became his signature tune.

THE SKATER'S WALTZ

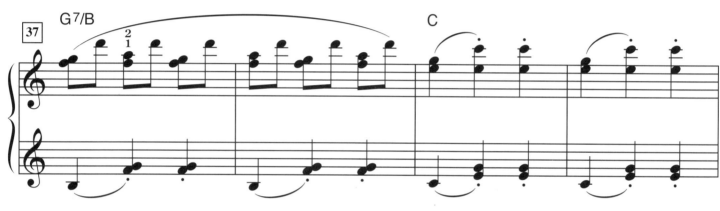

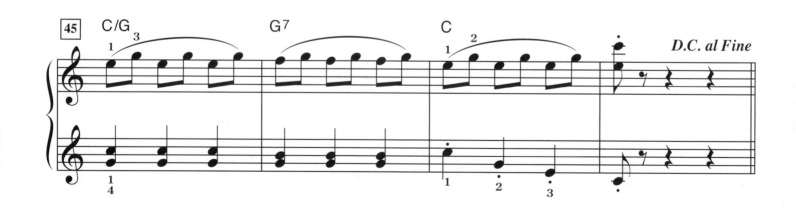

Johann Sebastian Bach was the greatest composer of the Baroque era. He turned out hundreds of compositions of all types: concertos, chamber music, keyboard music, and especially church music. A *cantata* is a vocal work for chorus, soloists and orchestra, often on religious subjects. The work that this excerpt comes from is called the *Birthday Cantata,* composed for a German nobleman's birthday celebration.

SHEEP MAY SAFELY GRAZE

Johann Sebastian Bach
(1685–1750)

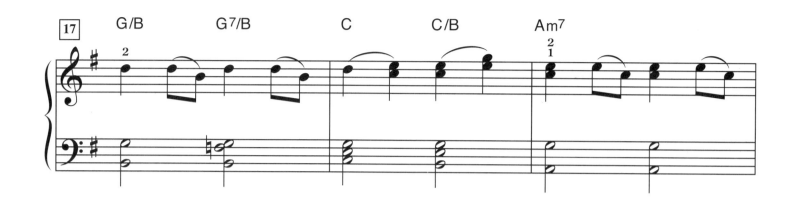

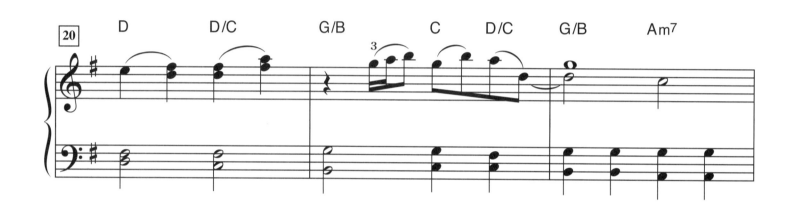

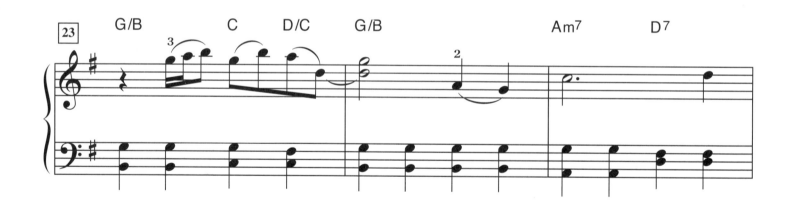

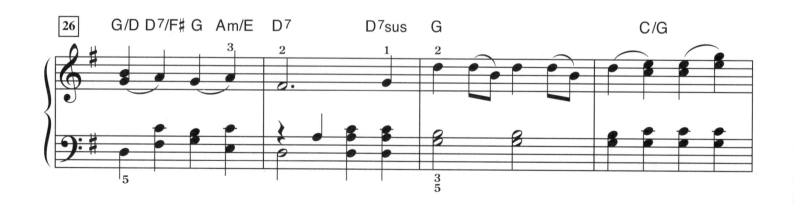

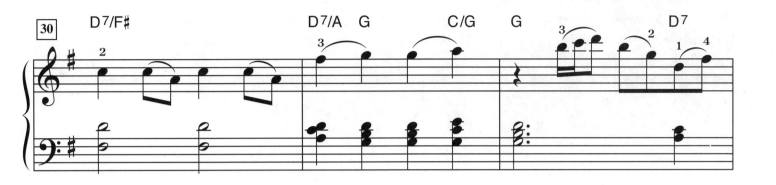

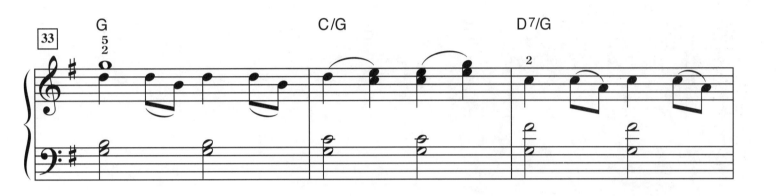

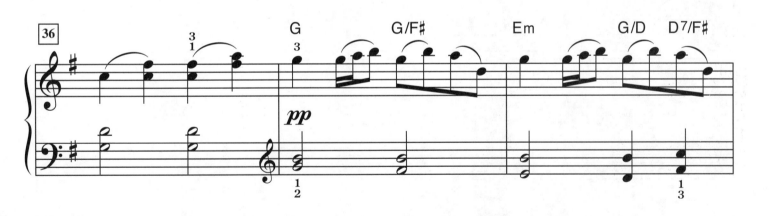

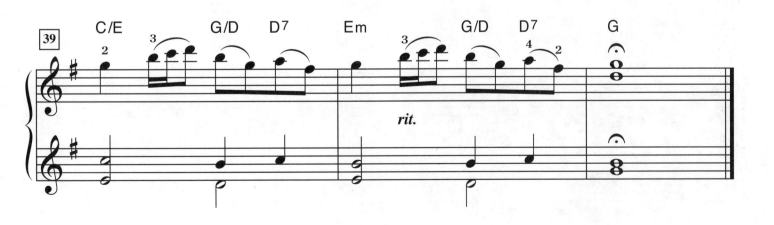

Russian composer Peter Ilyich Tchaikovsky was a master of melody, and arguably the most performed composer of the Romantic period. When Tchaikovsky was asked to create music for the ballet *Sleeping Beauty,* he was (as usual) in the depths of despair—but you'd never know it from the music he wrote for this charming ballet. Filled with beautiful melodies, the score is one of his most beloved.

SLEEPING BEAUTY
(Waltz Theme)

Peter Ilyich Tchaikovsky
(1840–1893)

The story of the sorcerer's apprentice, as told by Goethe, concerns a master magician and his lazy assistant. Given the job of carrying pails of water, the assistant uses magic to bring some brooms to life to take over his chores. However, chaos breaks out and the room becomes flooded! Only the timely arrival of the magician restores order. Using French composer Paul Dukas' score, Walt Disney brought the story to life in the 1940 movie *Fantasia,* with Mickey Mouse as the apprentice.

THE SORCERER'S APPRENTICE
(Main Theme)

Paul Dukas
(1865–1935)

Beloved Austrian composer Franz Joseph ("Papa") Haydn premiered this symphony in London in 1791. In the second movement, after 15 quiet measures of a very simple, almost child-like tune, the entire orchestra entered on a *fortissimo* (very loud) chord. The audience was so startled that many began to laugh, and since then, the symphony has been known as the "Surprise Symphony."

SURPRISE SYMPHONY

(2nd Movement Theme)

Franz Joseph Haydn
(1732–1809)

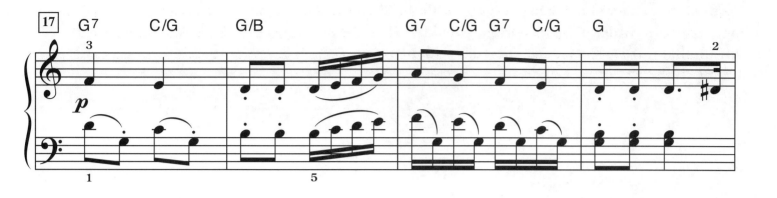

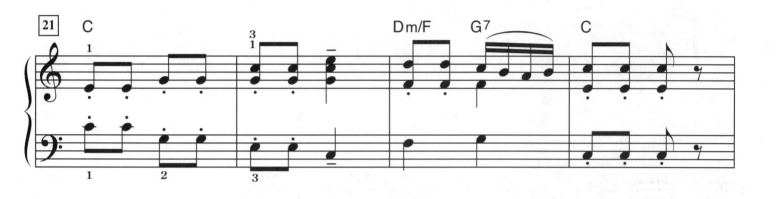

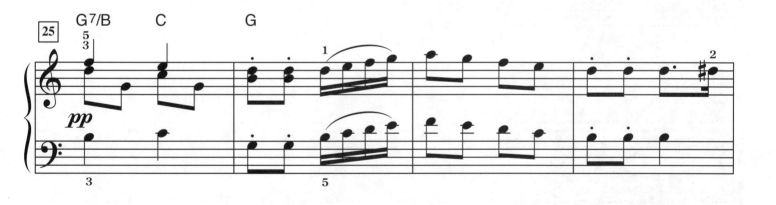

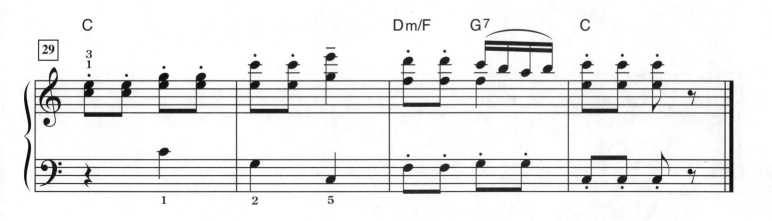

In Bizet's opera *Carmen,* a gypsy temptress entices the soldier Don José into abandoning the army and his sweetheart, Michaela. He runs away with Carmen to a gypsy encampment, but she soon tires of the soldier and instead takes up with the glamorous bullfighter, Escamillo. In this song, the macho torero brags about his bravery and the glamour of his profession. It was only after Bizet's death that *Carmen* became an incredibly popular opera.

TOREADOR SONG

(from *Carmen*)

Georges Bizet
(1838–1875)

Italian composer Antonio Vivaldi was one of the most prolific and important composers of the Baroque period. His group of concertos entitled *The Four Seasons,* written in the 1720s, is for solo violin and string orchestra. Of the four, *Spring* is the best known, and has been used in many films and television commercials.

SPRING

(from *The Four Seasons*)

Antonio Vivaldi
(1678–1741)

In Puccini's tragic masterpiece, Butterfly is a young Japanese girl who is seduced by a handsome American naval officer, Benjamin Franklin Pinkerton. He sails away leaving her pregnant, but promises to return. Three years pass and Butterfly sings yearningly about the "one fine day" when her lover will return. Pinkerton does return, but is accompanied by his American wife, and they've only come to take the baby away. In despair, Butterfly commits suicide.

UN BEL DÌ

(from *Madame Butterfly*)

Giacomo Puccini
(1858–1924)

Ordinarily the symphonies of the Late Classical to Early Romantic period contained four movements. Did Schubert intend for his Eighth Symphony to have only two movements? Or were the third and fourth movements lost? Or never completed? Nobody knows for sure, but the music in the two movements that we do have is so wonderful that this remains one of the most popular of the composer's symphonies.

THE UNFINISHED SYMPHONY
(1st Movement Theme)

Franz Schubert
(1797–1828)

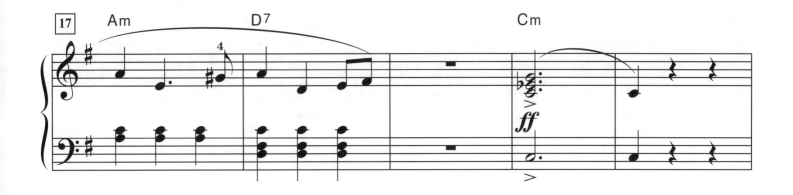

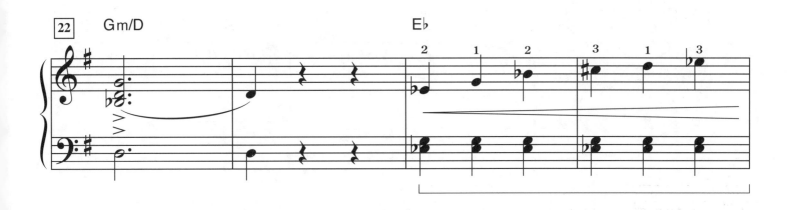

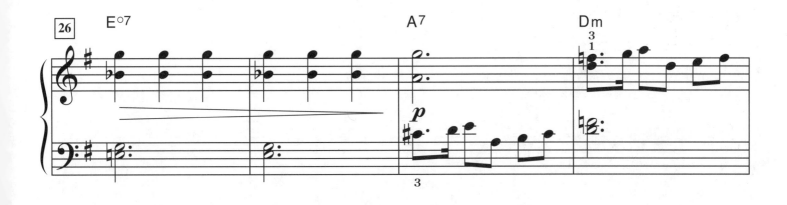

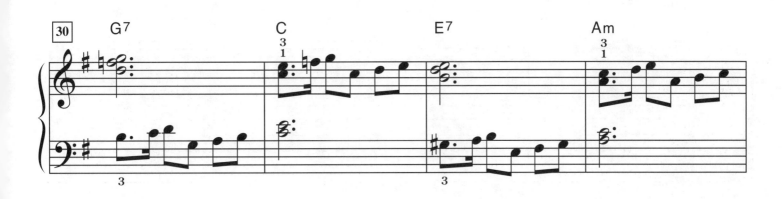

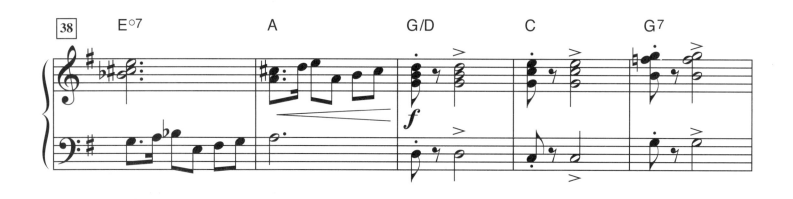

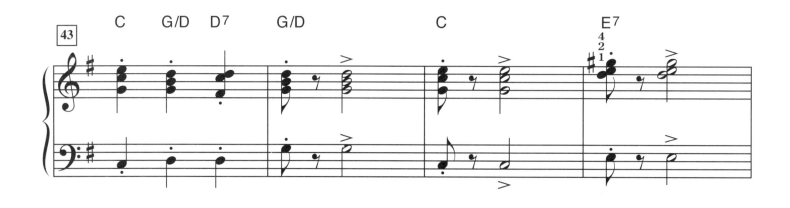

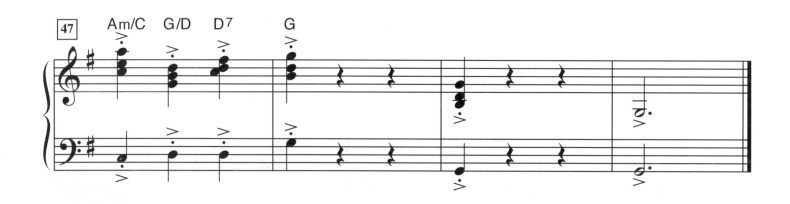

The first three of Tchaikovsky's symphonies are not often played nowadays, but his last three are extremely popular. Symphony No. 5, from which this excerpt is taken, is filled with beautiful melodies, and represents the composer at the height of his powers.

WALTZ
(from Symphony No. 5)

Peter Ilyich Tchaikovsky
(1840–1893)

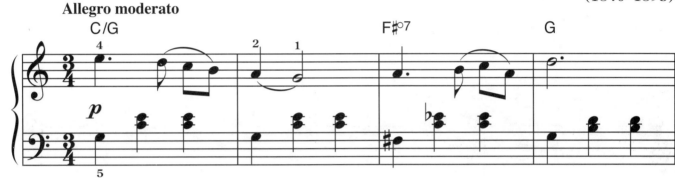

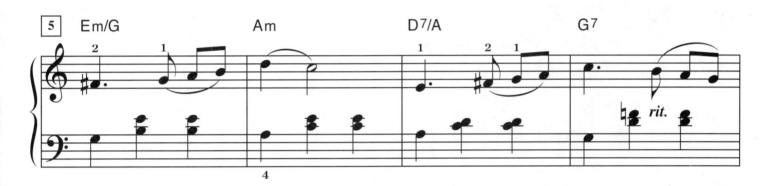

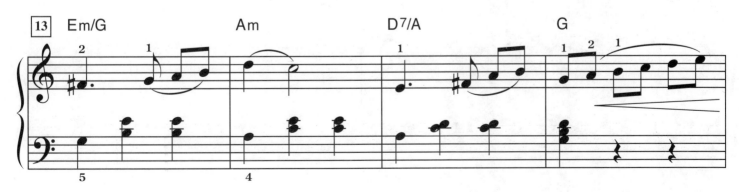

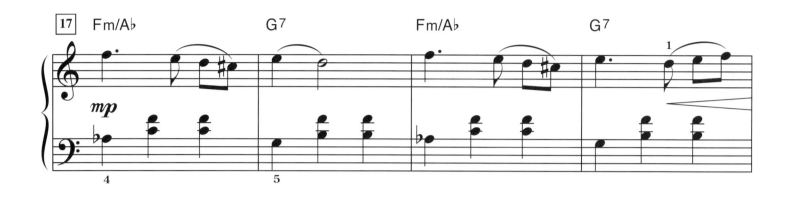

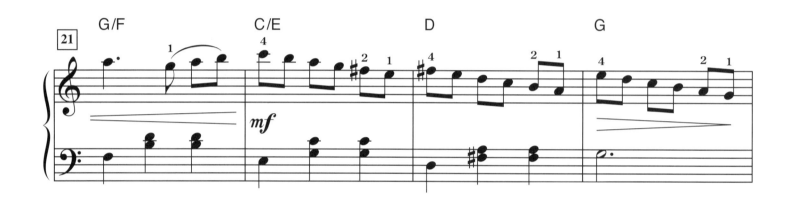

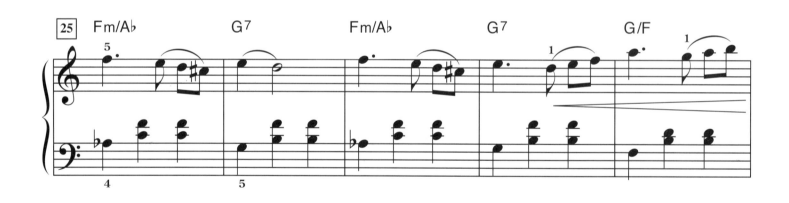

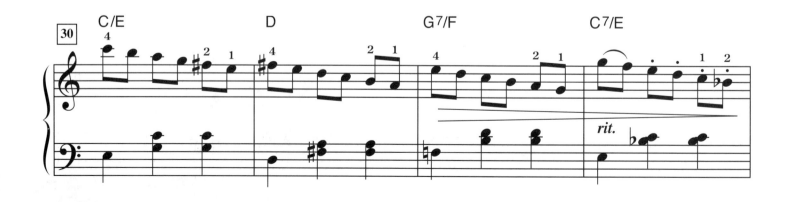

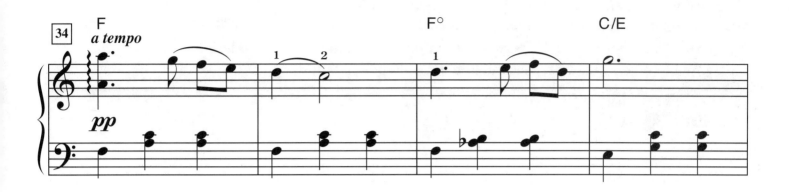

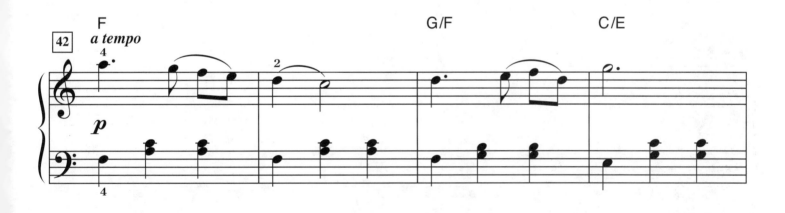

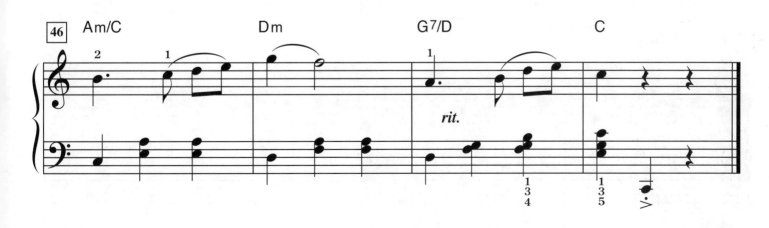

It's been said that the definition of an intellectual is somebody who can listen to the *William Tell Overture* without thinking of the Lone Ranger. Rossini's opera is about a legendary Swiss hero, William Tell, who is forced by a tyrannical governor to shoot an apple off his son's head with a bow and arrow. The opera was Rossini's last major work, coming after no less than 39 other operas, most of which were highly successful and are still played today.

WILLIAM TELL OVERTURE

Gioacchino Rossini
(1792–1868)

INDEX OF COMPOSERS AND THEIR WORKS